I'm Afraid of the Rain

I don't know why, but I'm afraid of the rain.

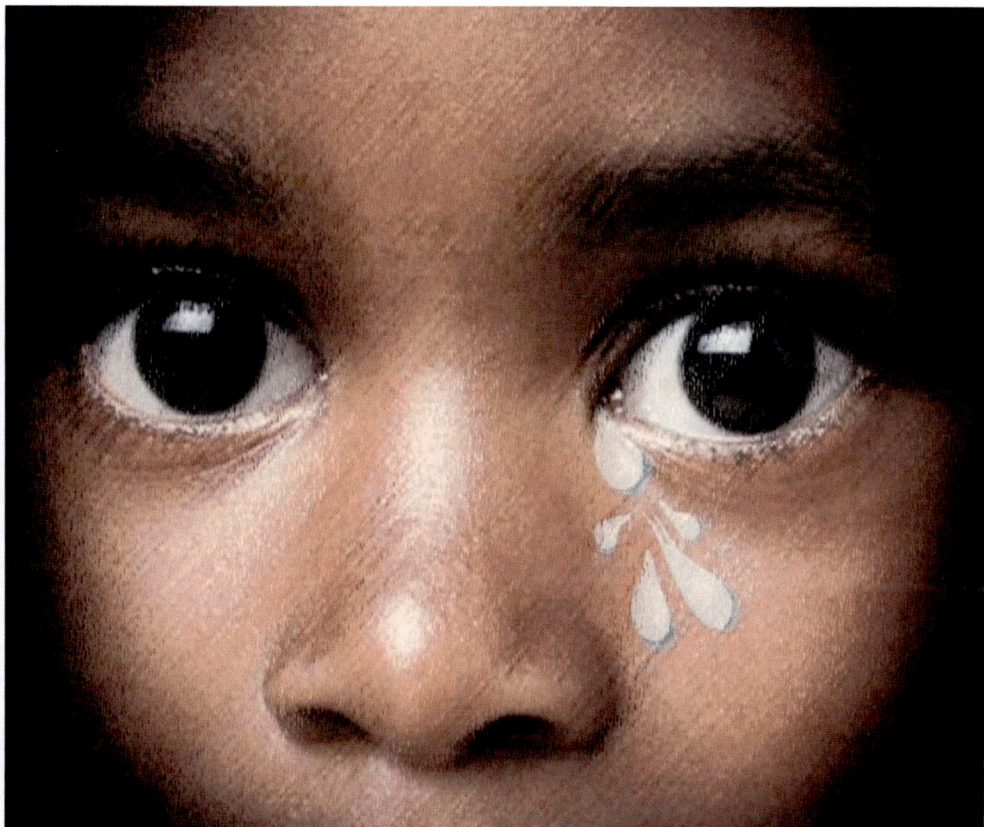

My tears drop when rain hits my window pane.

It's amazing because I am not afraid of anything, **BUT RAIN.**

I'm not afraid of a roller coaster.

Or the popping up of a toaster.

What I'm afraid
most of,
IS RAIN!

I'm not afraid to walk in the park after dark.

I have no fear of a BIG dog with a loud bark.

I'm not afraid of fireworks bangs and booms and bright sparks.

I wouldn't be afraid of tornadoes or hurricanes if they didn't come with all of that rain.

I'M AFRAID OF THE RAIN!!!

When I'm at the zoo and see a mean looking lion, I never start crying.

I simply say,
"Oh hush and be
quiet. Stop making a
riot."

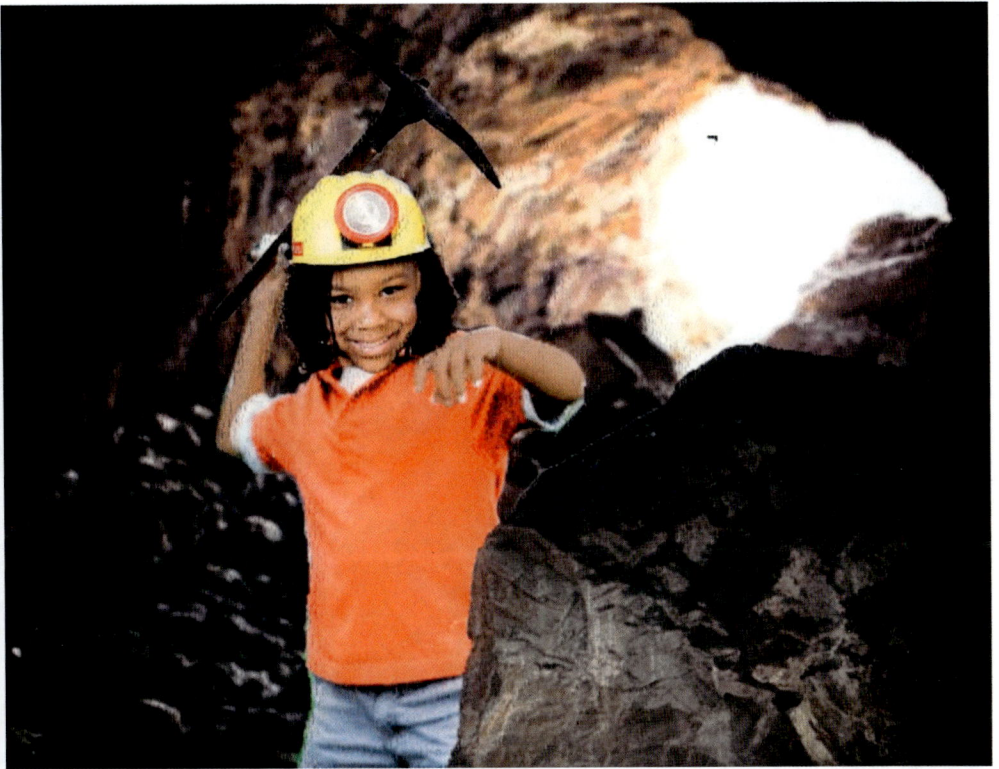

I'm not afraid to be on the tip top of a mountain top mining

I'm not afraid of heights.

I'm not afraid of flying in a plane.

And
I'm certainly
not afraid of
kites.

But for some reason... The reason I don't know.

I'm afraid of the rain you know.

Why?

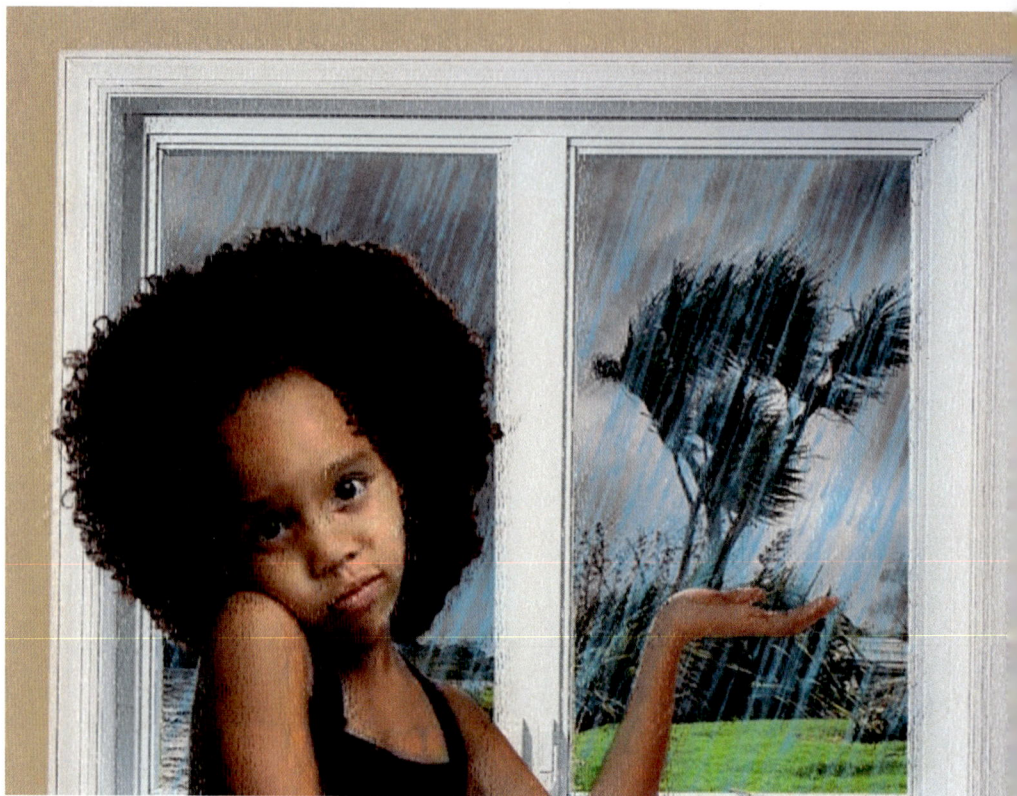

I said, *"I don't know."*
I never asked myself why.

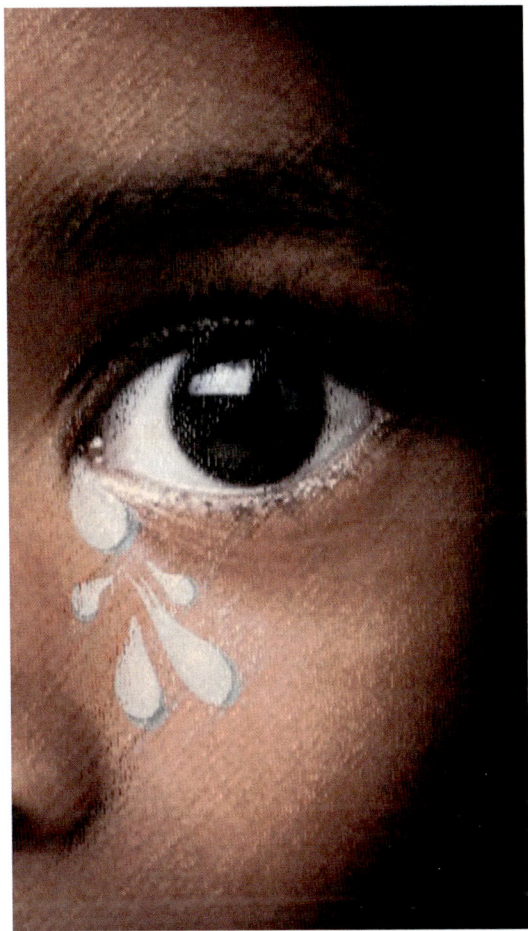

All I know is when it rains...
I BEGIN TO CRY.

BUT WHY?

Why do I cry when it rains?

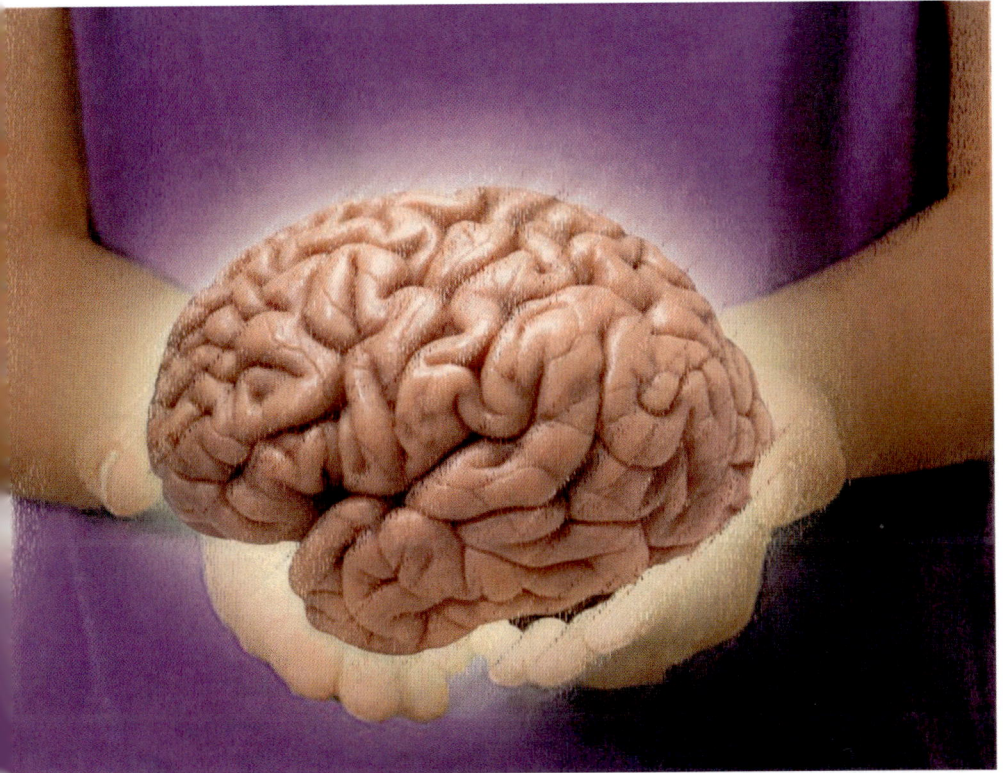

Hum!!!
Give me a second; let me look inside my brain.

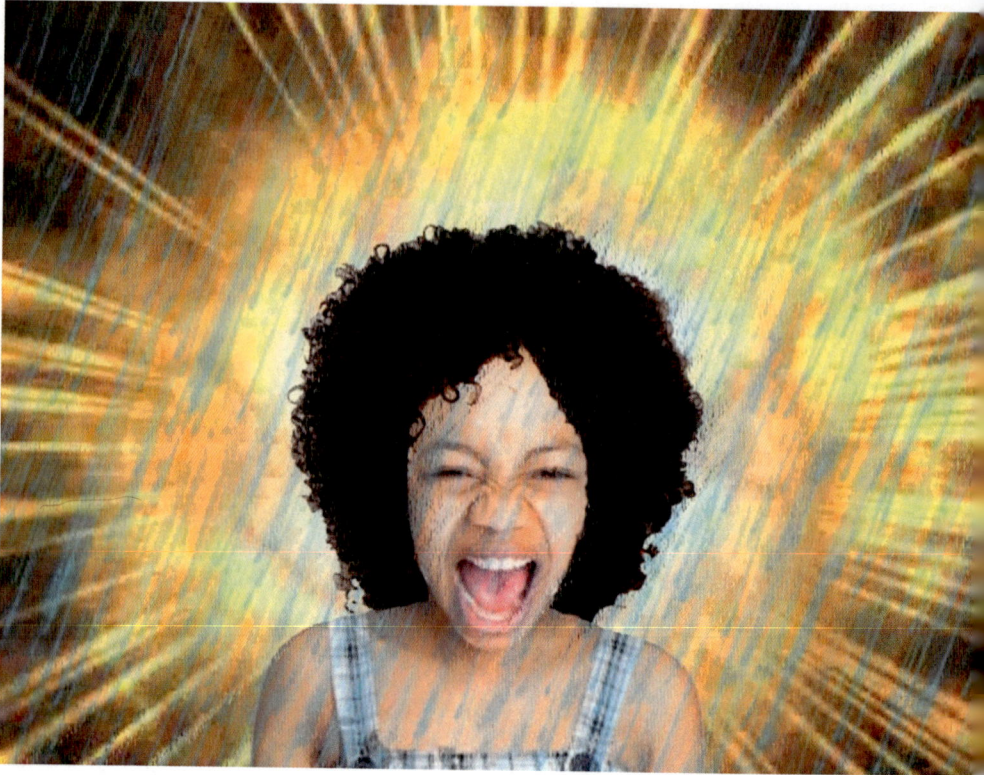

I know! I know!

The answer just came.

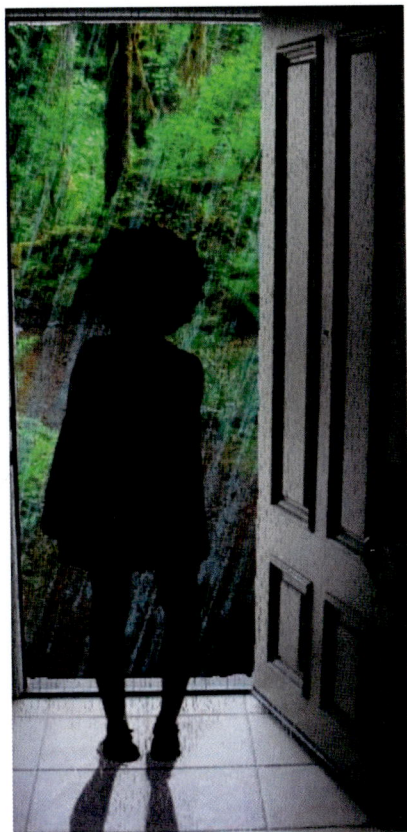

I'm afraid I won't go outside **EVER** again.

That's it!
That's it!

THAT'S WHY I'M AFRIAD OF THE RAIN!

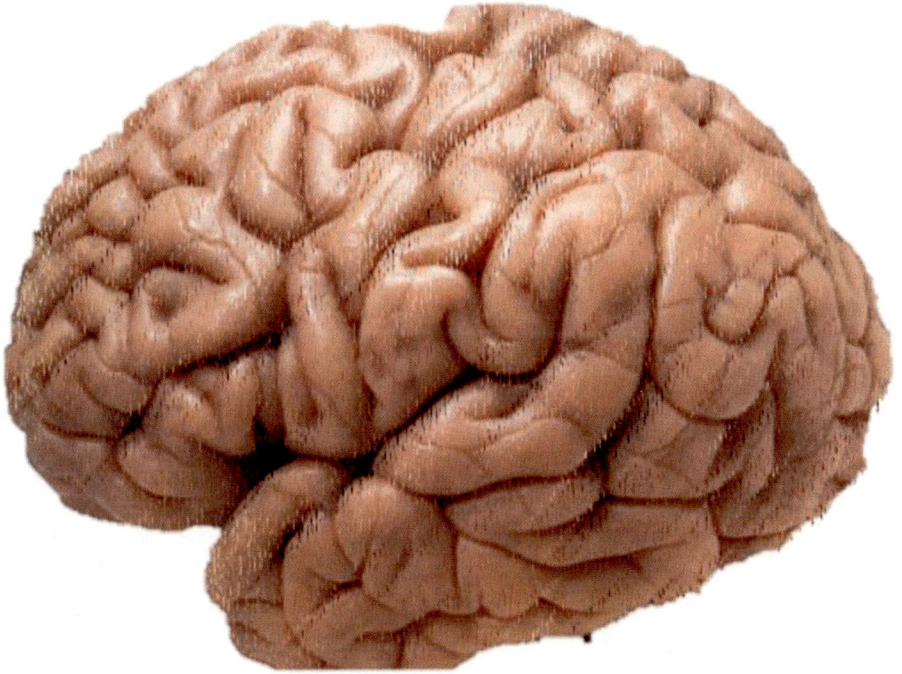

That was the silly reason hiding in my brain.

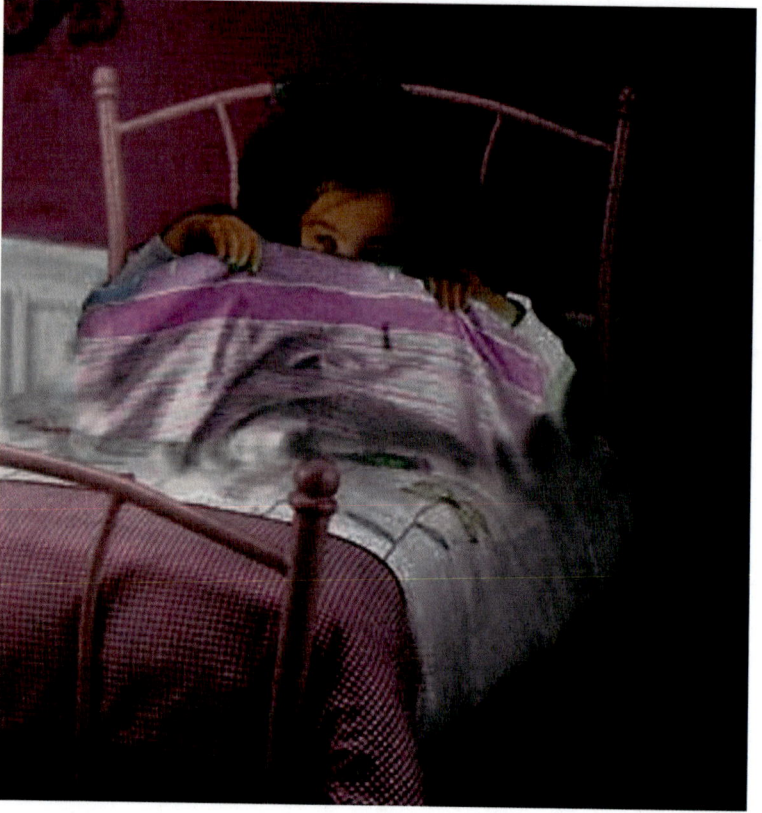

But now that I know why, that really is no reason to be afraid or to cry.

In fact,
I know it's
absolutely no
reason to cry.

Because every time it rains, it eventually stops and
I go back out again.

Well!

Well!

Well!

To put it simple and plain, I have no REAL reason to be afraid of the rain.

So starting today,

I'M NOT

AFRAID OF THE

RAIN

I'll cry no more tears and no more fear of the rain.

And since I'm not
afraid of anything
but rain, from this
day on

I'M NOT

AFRAID OF

ANYTHING!

I'm Afraid of the Rain

This book is dedicated to my daughter Chloe, the strongest, most resilent little lady that I know and to all the little girls and boys who read this book. I hope you find as much joy reading it as I did writing it.

To my my boys Jayden and Bryen. Thank you for being my inspiration and for giving me the opportunity to be your mom. Jerimiah, Niah, and Malya, my mom Sandra and my dad Stanley I love you very much....

I also dedicate this to my nieces, nephews, cousins, friends and family. Nate, Ashley, Zoe, Shun, Londyn, Brooklyn, Cameron, Justice, Journey, Makenzie, Malikie, Zion, Zackery, Kalema, Keira, Denea, Alana, Keyon, CeCe, Karie, Daniel, Shaquel, Myles, Myasia, and all of my babies that are too many to name but I love you all. Lastly, I dedicate this book to Thelma Johnson, Fannie Powell and Carter Johnson. Your legacy has made pain into passion possible and this book is for you.

Pain into Passion LLC (240) 245-7627

Made in the USA
Columbia, SC
17 May 2023